How to Maximize 24 Hours and Get More Done Effortlessly

Dr. Paris Love

How to Maximize 24 hours and Get More Done Effortlessly

How to Maximize 24 hours and Get More Done Effortlessly
© 2015-2025 by Dr. Paris Love

All rights reserved. Without limiting the rights under the copyright reserved above, no part of this publication many be reproduced, stored in or introduced into a retrieval system, or transmitted, in any form or by any means (electronic, mechanical, photocopying, recording, or otherwise), without the prior written permission of both the copyright owner and the publisher of this book.

The scanning, uploading, and distribution of this book via the Internet, or via any other means without the permission of the publisher is illegal and punishable by law. Please purchase only authorized electronic editions and do not participate in or encourage piracy of copyrightable materials. Your support of the author's right is appreciated.

ISBN-13: 978-1505655988
ISBN-10: 1505655986

Printed in the United States of America

Every effort has been made to make this book as complete and accurate as possible, but no warranty or fitness is implied. The information is provided in on an 'as is' basis. The author and the publisher shall have neither liability nor responsibility to any person or entity with respect to any loss or damages arising from the information contained in this book.

Any mention of a brand name or product or company should not be considered an endorsement of that product or company.

How to Maximize 24 hours and Get More Done Effortlessly

Also by Dr. Paris Love

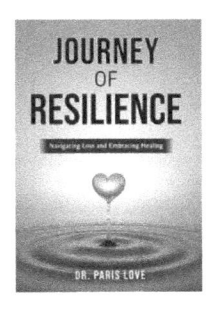

How to Maximize 24 hours and Get More Done Effortlessly

How to Maximize 24 hours and Get More Done Effortlessly

About the Author

With a career spanning over three decades, Dr. Paris Love is a nationally recognized productivity expert, bestselling author, and dedicated community leader. Known as "The Drill Sergeant of Productivity," she has transformed countless lives by helping professionals and businesses streamline their operations and achieve greater success.

Dr. Love is a former U.S. Army Sergeant whose military discipline and leadership have shaped her approach to coaching and organizing. Her professional accomplishments include founding **Paris Love Productivity Institute**, which has thrived for more than 20 years, focusing on helping clients overcome mental, physical, and emotional clutter to unlock their full potential.

Dr. Love's literary achievements include publishing 13 books, and receiving Amazon's top 100 Best Sellers in two categories and the TAZ award for her novel, Growing Pains. She has been featured on FEMI Magazine, Focus Atlanta, CW Atlanta, My Atlanta TV, and OnlineOrganizing. She is also a seasoned speaker featured on platforms and multiple **podcasts,** sharing her expertise with diverse audiences.

She holds advanced degrees in Human Resources and Business Administration, a doctorate in Advanced Studies of Human Behavior, and certifications as a NaVOBA-certified service disabled veteran-owned business. With accolade and numerous business honors, Dr. Love exemplifies excellence, resilience, and a commitment to empowering others.

How to Maximize 24 hours and Get More Done Effortlessly

Table of Contents

The book is divided into five different sections providing you helpful tips and solutions for maximizing your time so you get more done effortlessly. You will also find advice from several productivity experts sprinkled throughout.

Part I. How - To Get Started   8
   Forget resolutions and set positive intentions   8
   How to take control and stay the course   14
   How to work solo   18
   How to analyze and make mid-year adjustments   23

Part II. Attitude   28
   It really is in your head   28
   Motivation   31
   No person is an island   35
   How to get inspiration when you most need it   37
   Work through uncertainty   43

Part III. Time Management   46
   Email   46
   Knowing when to let go   53
   Hourglass and Internet   56
   Stick to your goals when everything is important   61

Part IV. Staying Organized   66
   Paper Filing   66
   What's getting in your way   72

How to Maximize 24 hours and Get More Done Effortlessly

Office messes	75
Pros, cons and quick tips for your "Time Style"	77

Part V. Keeping a Healthy You   80
Work Life Balance   80
Work hard, play hard, sleep fast   83
Priorities   86
Delegation might save the day - and you   90

How to Maximize 24 hours and Get More Done Effortlessly

How -To Get Started

Forget about must do resolutions – set positive intentions!

Ahhhhh. The sweetness of completing your to do list every day. Feels good, doesn't it? What's that? You don't get all your tasks completed? Feel discouraged? Don't have a 'to-do' list at all? At the risk of committing "Eastwooding" (talking to an empty chair), now's the time when you might expect I would tell you to get going on your to do list, make one, write it down and then attack it.

But no. I'm going to start with a bigger picture. January is the perfect month for big picture planning, because we have this whole New Year in front of us, a sense of completion from last year, and a renewed energy. Many use this energy and fresh year to make resolutions, which are generally promptly ignored couple of weeks later. Resolution has this sort of commanding connotation and we tend to resist being told what to do, even if and sometimes especially if we are doing the telling to ourselves.

Start with a big picture plan
Instead, I'm presenting you with some optional actions you can take to get your big picture plan created for the year that will result in helping you decide what to do each quarter, month, week and day – actions that are in alignment with what you want, keep you focused and feed your motivation.

I once heard an unattributed quote: "Obstacles are what we see when we take our eyes of the goal." You can have obstacles with or

How to Maximize 24 hours and Get More Done Effortlessly

without a goal, but I'm betting you'll get through, around and over them a lot easier if you know where you're headed.

Choose three to five major areas of your life where you anticipate or want change.
For example, maybe you are planning to relocate this year, or perhaps you want to get fit or get a promotion or grow a business you are leading. It could be a spiritual, mental, physical or environmental change.

Set your intentions.
"I intend to make my move this year as easy and pleasurable as possible."

"I intend to grow my business with a 20% increase in net revenue this year."

"I intend to try one exciting thing this year I've never done before."

"I intend to improve my relationship with my partner."

Define how you will go about supporting your intentions. Be specific.

"I intend to make my move this year as easy and pleasurable as possible by getting help, making a packing plan and viewing the move as a positive exploration experience."

or

"I intend to grow my business with a 20% increase in net revenue this year by introducing three new products and cutting costs."

How to Maximize 24 hours and Get More Done Effortlessly

For each quarter of the year, make a list of the supporting actions you defined above. For the first quarter of the year, in the moving example, you might list:
Schedule my move
Call a moving company or other moving help
Pack one room each week (or two rooms a month)
Find a moving checklist online

Translate your quarterly list into monthly, weekly and daily activities.

In the business growth example it might look like this:
January: Conceptualize three new products
Gather financials for cost cutting review
Schedule product introductions

February: Create first new product
Review financials and identify potential cost cuts
Create a repeatable product launch plan

Every week, review your monthly list, pick which item(s) to do, and then plan which day you will accomplish these.

Yes, I know that you also have daily and maintenance activities to schedule as well and you'll make room in your schedule for them without getting LOST in the land of to-do's that don't make a difference. By creating set intentions, you avoid making commitments that don't serve you, and you have the power to decide on how many intentions and the depth of them so you still control your use of time.

More importantly, your intentions and subsequent intended actions support what you want, help you feel accomplished, and move you closer to living the life you want.

Obstacles are what you see when you take your eyes off the goal.

How to Maximize 24 hours and Get More Done Effortlessly

But first you need to have a goal. Every day we are faced with small and sometimes large obstacles, and we attack them or become discouraged. Here's the thing: many of the problems that come up daily you DON'T have to deal with – only do so when it's getting in the way of what you have intended to accomplish for the year. For example, if you intend to get a promotion, don't allow yourself to get distracted with petty office gossip or worry about being gossiped about. Stay focused on your goal and take a positive action to reach it, such as asking your boss how you can better support him or her.

A plane flying around without a destination is bound to run out of gas.
A person without a plan doesn't have a destination.
Therefore…well, you get the picture. Setting intentions and making a flight plan to support you getting there is critical to everyday life satisfaction, productivity, and creating the life you really want. Without at least a rough outline of a plan, you are leaving your life up to chance alone. While plans don't always work out, having one gives you better odds of arriving before you run out of fuel.

Plan for serendipity
Remember the old joke about the man marooned in the ocean praying to God for help? Along comes boat, a helicopter and a rescue team, but the man refuses them because he doesn't see them as God's direct help. When you set your intentions for the year, and create a supportive plan for yourself, remember to keep your eyes open for serendipitous opportunities to further your plan or take you there via a different route.

Make a doable 'to-do' list
No matter how tempted, keep your Daily To-Do list short. Set yourself up for success by ensuring you can actually accomplish what you planned. Ask yourself, what absolutely HAS to get completed TODAY? It helps if you are working from a monthly or weekly plan first, so you can anticipate what's important. It's not

How to Maximize 24 hours and Get More Done Effortlessly

fun to go to bed every night thinking about what you didn't accomplish.

Stop! Time for a brain dump.
Here's a tip for when your brain is overflowing with things to do and creating anxiety for you: Stop and do a brain dump. Take a piece of paper or computer screen, and write down every single thing that comes into your head that you feel you want or need to do. EVERYTHING, including personal stuff like sending Aunt Edith a get well card, groceries you need, work assignments. No order required. Just keep going until you can't think of another single thing. You'll know you're done because you will feel a sense of relief – there it is, all laid out for you and you no longer have to keep it in your head. Follow up by organizing the items on the list by category, such as Personal, Work, Maybe Someday, and Urgent. Then create your daily to do list.

How to Maximize 24 hours and Get More Done Effortlessly

How to take control and stay the course

Any of these work avoidance scenarios sound familiar?

You're working but get an urge to get something sweet to eat and off to the kitchen or vending machine you go

You're working from home and decide it's time to take the dog out for a walk or clean the kitchen

You get caught up along the Internet highway and when you finally exit, a couple hours have gone by

You can't find the right size paperclip so decide to clean out your top desk drawer NOW

You suddenly remember you need to call your friend about the weekend plans and end up in a long conversation

You sometimes wonder if what you are doing is (a)valuable (b) worth it (c) good enough (d) all of the above

You don't have to have ADHD to find yourself seriously off course – it's common for human beings to be pulled away voluntarily or involuntarily from the goal directed task at hand or your to do list no matter how much you love your profession, for a number of reasons:
- Parts of your job or business just aren't enjoyable
- Big projects feel overwhelming and create inertia
- You're not getting enough input or reward for your efforts
- Fear of success, failure, or both
- There's something you have to do but are dreading it, like firing your assistant

How to Maximize 24 hours and Get More Done Effortlessly

- You just don't feel like working on a particular day

The result of continually being off course from what it takes to accomplish your goals is insidious and has a wide ripple effect. That one task you didn't accomplish today because you were walking the dog during your scheduled work time affects the next task, and the next. Pretty soon the deadline is here and you aren't even close to being ready.

There are ways to take control and stay the course, even when you'd rather be outside on the hammock. Try these seven tips to keep yourself going in the right direction and move closer to the success of accomplishing your goals this year:

- **Call it like it is:** You know when you are avoiding, and even more, you know what you are avoiding. Stop whatever non-essential work or task you are doing and clarify why you have taken the side road. Write it down if you need to: "Cleaning out my desk drawer is my way of avoiding getting started on my next product launch because I am overwhelmed by it."
- **What's the worst that could happen?:** Ask yourself what are the consequences of not getting started on your project when planned? Will you miss deadlines for yourself and others? If it's your own business, how does that affect the bottom line? If you work for a business, how will it affect your performance rating? If it's a home organization project, will delaying make it worse or better?
- **Check your mindset:** Most of the time the consequences of not doing something affect your psyche – how you feel about yourself. "If I didn't get my work done today, I can be mighty grouchy this evening" or "If my product launch doesn't happen on time, I will lose valuable clients and

How to Maximize 24 hours and Get More Done Effortlessly

income and my business will fail and I will be a failure." Resetting your thought process can make a huge difference: "I got most of my work done today and I'll tackle the rest tomorrow" or "I am going to do what it takes to keep my product launch on target." How you talk to yourself is critical to reaching your goals – or abandoning them.

- **Talk it out:** Especially when you are working on a project or task by yourself, talking to a friend or colleague can really help re-motivate you to keep on it. You gain clarity just be speaking with someone who is willing to listen. But don't get sidetracked into unrelated conversation.
- **Put yourself on a timer:** Those old kitchen timers can be a super tool when you are in avoidance mode. Tell yourself you will work on this project for one hour (or whatever you can tolerate), set the timer, and get to work. Knowing there is an end helps you to have boundaries around the task which in turn helps you get something meaningful accomplished.
- **Cross it off your list:** If you have something on your to do list for more than a month and you've done nothing to get closer to crossing it off your list, then cross it off your list. Really. Projects we let languish and continue to avoid aren't worth stewing over. Likely you gave yourself some arbitrary work that you thought was a good idea at the time – but not good enough to actually work on.
- **Look at the big picture:** Lack of motivation and getting off course can often occur because we are lost in the day to day task abyss and lose sight of our long term goals and the benefits of reaching these goals. Get out your annual goal list and review where you want to be by the end of this year,

How to Maximize 24 hours and Get More Done Effortlessly

and then ensure that every task on your list is directly or indirectly getting you there.

How to Maximize 24 hours and Get More Done Effortlessly

How to work solo

You start your own business because you want the freedom of making the decisions and doing it your way. You get to create your own brand, your programs, your plan, your schedule and your life. There's only one thing missing. The boss. Remember those days where you worked in a J-O-B and your boss set the priorities? Whether you liked your boss or not, at least you knew what was expected and someone held you *accountable*.

Picture this and see if it sounds familiar:

You start your day at whatever time works for you. The phone calls begin business and personal. The kitchen calls to you that it's time for a snack. You have a mid-day personal thing, like the kids school pick up, or a medical appointment. While you are working on your emails, you click a link that catches your attention and before you know it an hour more has passed. You answer several e-mails, make a few changes to your website. Meanwhile, that important service, product or program you are developing sits and waits….. again.

You've accomplished some things for sure, but not much that will move you forward.

Two key strategies are missing in this picture: Focus and Accountability. Since now you are your own boss with only yourself to answer to, you can give yourself time off, become easily distracted by whatever comes your way, and lose focus. Unless you are an expert at self-discipline, it's tough to be productive, meet your personally set deadlines, or set priorities without some sort of outside pressure to push you forward.

How to Maximize 24 hours and Get More Done Effortlessly

Holding yourself accountable is often a blind side for solopreneurs because...

- left to our own devices, we tend to pick the small easy tasks to do first, before moving on to a larger project or a task we fear or don't really like to do.
- big projects seem overwhelming, so it's easy to feel more of a sense of accomplishment by tackling the little ones first.
- since we have the power to set our deadlines, we also have the power to extend them or not meet them at all. And why not? Who's watching?
- human beings are easily distracted by just about everything around them, especially in a technologically wild world
- without positive reinforcement it is very easy to become discouraged, dissatisfied and to feel higher levels of stress and frustration.
- it's also easy to become isolated from colleagues, peers, clients and customers, which leads to poor decision making in a vacuum.

Getting focused and becoming accountable when you're working on your own on a business or even a personal project or goal is about finding the right support through an expert coach or regularly scheduled colleague meetings or even by creating your own advisory board.

Despite your commitment, working on your to do list every day, and maybe even on the weekends, it's easier by far to accomplish your goals with support, encouragement, action planning and accountability.

How to Maximize 24 hours and Get More Done Effortlessly

Coaches and self-formed advisory boards can help you:
- determine and set your priorities
- develop an action plan around each priority
- keep you focused on your plan
- set completion dates
- overcome obstacles that come up as you work toward your goals
- gather and give helpful feedback on your plans, goals and strategy
- partner with you, cheer you on, support your efforts and hold you accountable
- Being the real deal working as your own boss also means making the important responsibility of investing in ways to hold yourself accountable.

You are the boss of you!

Did you know there are coaches who can help you remain accountable to yourself in your business endeavor or projects by providing you with help to set your priorities, create an action plan with completion dates, overcome obstacles and give you feedback? That's because solopreneurs (actually almost everybody!) has a natural tendency to need that extra push from outside themselves. Just as a boss in business learns to motivate her employees, your job as your own boss is to constantly motivate... YOU.

The right partner makes it work
Choose a accountability partner and make agreements to meet regularly and keep each other on track – you'll be amazed at how much more you'll accomplish! Select a colleague you respect, who understands the work you do, who won't let you off the hook easily and who will also support your efforts and celebrate your accomplishments. Then be prepared to do the same for your partner.

How to Maximize 24 hours and Get More Done Effortlessly

Even the CEO is accountable to the Board
When it comes to accountability, even the highest level CEO is accountable to the Board of Directors and the shareholders. If you work on your own, your clients can help to hold you accountable because you don't want to let them down for a number of reasons: integrity, supporting your clients, your professionalism, and your business reputation. Even if you are at a place where you are still working on building a client base, remember that there are people out there looking for exactly what you can offer.

Ask the right questions when you are stuck
Struggling with holding yourself accountable when it comes to your work or a project you have on your to do list? Ask yourself these questions:

- Why is this job on my to do list? Clarifying purpose can motivate you.
- What is the direct benefit to me of getting this work completed? Will you feel relieved, joyous?
- What is the value to others of me doing this project? Who is missing out because your new program isn't developed?
- How will my life be changed by crossing this item off my list? Maybe more time for friends and family, business growth?

Use these questions when you get stuck on a project, program, service or business task to spur yourself on.

Trite but true: start with the tough stuff
This isn't new but it bears repetition: begin your day not with the small, easy tasks, but with the tough ones. You have more energy at the start of the day and by doing the stuff you don't love early on, you have cleared your day so you can do what you do love. Same for large projects. Start working on it right away so you don't keep putting it off. These ways of holding yourself accountable can move

How to Maximize 24 hours and Get More Done Effortlessly

you forward much more quickly and make each day a whole lot more pleasurable.

Tell the world about it
Hold yourself accountable in your work when you are an entrepreneur can be tough. One way to deal with it is to announce your intention(s) to everyone you know: on Facebook, in your newsletter, to your friends and family. That way you get support and a whole lot of people you are now accountable to!

How to Maximize 24 hours and Get More Done Effortlessly

How to analyze and make mid-year adjustments

It's in those lazy, hazy, crazy days of summer that you can set aside some time to reflect on how your lives and businesses have been doing in this past year, and make necessary course adjustments. Take your pad (paper or computer) outside on the deck, porch, hammock or bench with a long tall glass of something cool, and ask yourself these ten questions. This is a great journaling exercise, or you can just take reminder notes as you reflect. You'll hone in on just what's working and what's not, along with giving yourself a chance to celebrate your progress and reflect on what's important to you!

What did my life and/or business look like a year ago today? List briefly how you were doing financially, spiritually, on relationships, personal development, family, and business growth a year ago. Perspective is what you are going for here. It's easy to get caught up in your daily to do's, hectic lives, and demands on your time, then be discouraged when you don't get all twenty things on your list accomplished.

What has changed since last year? Now take a look at what's changed in those areas of your life. For example, "business income increased about 20%" or "much improved relationship with sister." Then take a moment to reflect on and celebrate what you feel has changed positively. A constant focus on the future doesn't give you time to recognize just how far you've come. For areas where you don't perceive any change or feel the change has negatively affected you, ask yourself what you'd like to do about it in a perfect world. Make notes as you can use this information in upcoming mid-year review questions.

What would I like my life to look like in a year from today? Look into the future and imagine what you want to be different,

How to Maximize 24 hours and Get More Done Effortlessly

improved, changed in the major areas of your life by this time next year. "I envision hiring a team to help with my growing business so I have more free time" or "I want to spend more quality time with my spouse or partner" are examples. Take your time on this one, because you are painting the picture of your life in a year. Be realistic but stretch a little, too.

What will it take for me to get where I want to be? Decide what exactly you need to do to get to your vision for a year from today. If your plan is to be more productive in your business and life by working smarter, not harder, just what do you need to make that happen? (hint... a productivity coach is one idea). Maybe you picture yourself in a year sitting on a beach doing yoga. What's the next step that you can take this week to get started?

How have I been doing against my annual plan for these first six months of the year? Have you taken steps toward reaching those goals? If yes, celebrate; if not, why? If you can quantify, go ahead and do so: "I am about halfway toward this goal with a solid plan for the rest of the year" or "I have completed 10% of the work on this project." No judgment necessary - you are simply reporting on your progress toward goal completion for coming year.

What has been working well this year, and what has not? Answering this question is a super opportunity to specifically explore each goal. Perhaps you are right on target with your spiritual and personal development goals, yet your business goal progress is slower. Ask yourself why. It might be avoidance, it could be the goal is unreachable and therefore discouraging, or it could be that you are facing a personal obstacle. Taking the time to examine the why's behind your progress toward goals helps you breakthrough whatever has been standing in your way.

What changes do I want to make in my annual plan and goals to align with my long term goals? There may be goals that need to be revamped, eliminated or you will add some of the goals you

How to Maximize 24 hours and Get More Done Effortlessly

envisioned when you pictured where you want to be in a year. It's OK to cross a goal or objective off your annual list if it has become irrelevant or moved down on the priority list. Also OK to add new goals that are aligned with your personal vision of where you want to be in a year.

How do I feel about my progress toward my goals and why? Qualification is a good thing. Yet much of why you do or do not reach goals is about you. It has to do with real and perceived obstacles, self-motivation, self-respect, wellbeing, fears (of both failure and success), aversion to change, and desire to grow. By experiencing your feelings about how you are doing so far this year, you are giving yourself a chance to reflect, sort out what is real and what is self-created, which then gives you the clarity to see just what you can do about it.

What can I do differently for the remainder of this year? OK, you know where you were, where you want to be, where you stand against this year's goals, you've adjusted and synched your goals with your vision and you've figured out what is getting in your way. Now you can figure out next steps. If your goal is to be more productive in building your business, one statement you can make might be "I will not spend my whole morning on emails – instead I will give it one hour then move onto income producing tasks." "I am going to finish that chapter in my book even if it's not perfect," is your next step toward writing your book is you are finding yourself to be a perfectionist.

What will have to shift in me in order for me to meet my yearly goals? Mindset is always the answer to this question. Mindset shift is different for everyone, but by answering the previous nine questions, you will have a better feel for how your thinking and outlook can shift so that you can create the life you envision. Changing mindset requires some personal "stick-to-it" quality AND the ability to know when you need help and support.

How to Maximize 24 hours and Get More Done Effortlessly

Screen save your annual goals
Want to stay on track for with your goals? Try reading them at least once a week (every morning is even better) so that you train your mind to stay focused and send out your intent to the universe. Give yourself acknowledgement for what you have done toward your goals. I've even seen clients create a document that becomes the screen saver for their computers, listing their annual goal. By keeping your objectives front and center, you are able to ask yourself about every task you do: "Is this a task that is helping me reach my goals?"

Challenge yourself to ask for support
No man is an island is an oft repeated cliché for good reason. No one reaches their own life goals alone. Even the recluse in the woods needs mother nature's gifts. When you review your goals for this year, remember to ask for support from your higher power, coach, friends and family on those goals that are proving to be more of a challenge. Sometimes just a discussion with a colleague can create the breakthrough you need to move forward. Isolation is deadly to our creative thought process – reach out.

Need a mindset makeover?
 Frequently, because you are human, anxiety or fears pop up that show themselves as negativity, get you stuck in one way of thinking, or narrow your perspective. All of these stifle your creativity and can be discouraging. The best part of this scenario is that you have the power to change the way you think. By shifting to positivity, brainstorming, and a broadened perspective that includes gratitude, you powerfully open your mind and heart so that what once seemed insurmountable now appears as simply an opportunity for growth.

Figure out your BIG WHY
Set some super long term goals. A friend of mine had annual goals, both personal and professional, but she also had five year and lifetime objectives. She wanted to visit every continent in her

How to Maximize 24 hours and Get More Done Effortlessly

lifetime (she has made four out of seven and is still working on it). Writing a book was another of her long term goals and she tells me the research is complete. She wants to be on the board of directors of a major charity. These BIG and long term goals motivate her to complete the monthly and annual goals she sets – they are her big "why". Having that big why is what drives you toward goals and keeps you motivated.

Try a "Core Dump"

When you get overwhelmed, try the "core dump" exercise. Sit down in a quiet place with pen and paper, take three deep breaths, then write down every single thing in your brain that you want to do. No classifying, just dump it all out of your head onto the paper. These can be things to do today, tomorrow, next week, next year and five years from now – just everything you can possible think of. Keep writing until you can't think of any more to add. Take another deep breath and relax because you now have it all on paper and you don't have to juggle it all in your head anymore. When you are ready, go ahead and separate your list by category, then ask yourself what absolutely HAS to be done today (be honest). And don't forget to examine your list against your annual goals and see how much of what you have listed is just busy work that won't get you any closer to where you want to be.

How to Maximize 24 hours and Get More Done Effortlessly

Attitude

It really IS all in your head

Whether you view it as the law of attraction, the power of positive thinking, affirmation statements, or optimistic thinking, your mindset is more of a determinant of your health and wellbeing than you might imagine.

In fact, there's plenty of evidence that how you think affects your relationships, happiness quotient and your work or business.
It's a pretty simple premise that you hear at a young age when the little engine that could –does, simply by believing. When the ever bright Pollyanna turns around scads of naysayers simply with her positive outlook, you want to cheer.

Yet it works that way in our lives, too. The self-defeating prophecy, the one where you say "I don't think I can do it" brings about just that result – you don't do it, whatever it is.

Today, popular entrepreneurial and big business motivational speakers hinge their talks on the idea of mindset, so there's lots of good stuff out there to draw from when it comes to developing a positive, I- know- I- can- attitude – one that pulls you through when the curve balls start heading your way.

Since mindset is basically a set of thoughts, attitudes and beliefs that effect how you respond to and interpret situations, you have a particular power that no one else has: you can change the way you think, what you believe and how you approach life and work.

How to Maximize 24 hours and Get More Done Effortlessly

The challenge happens when it comes to just how to make this shift, but it turns out the field of psychology has already figured this out. Your brain will respond to your actions. Hence if you print and post beliefs you want to hold, such as "I am the leader of a prosperous business", you will eventually believe it and the result is likely to become what you believe.

Or, if you wake up every day and say to yourself "I have so much to do, I am so stressed", you're going to spend the day feeling and being stressed, which will negatively impact your performance. On the other hand, if you think "I choose to be stress free today" you find a way to manage your day that makes your life easier and your heart lighter.

I've rounded up thoughts on how to give yourself the gift of a mindset that can mean the life you want vs. the life you settle for:

Fill your life with positive people: Ever been around a person who complains, whines, is negative about everything? This type of person will drain your energy, rob your positivity. Instead, surround yourself with those who support you, your efforts, and your decisions and for whom you can do the same.

Add a dose of inspiration: Books, quotes, podcasts, even some music can be uniquely and positively inspiring. Seek these out. Try to incorporate it into your life every day.

Create a plan: Long term, short term, quarterly, monthly, weekly, daily – whatever works for you. Having even a loose plan can help you to have purpose each day, know what you are doing and why, and give immediate positive feedback as you cross items off your list.

Practice exquisite self-care: It's been studied and proven that lack of adequate sleep, a diet full of sugar and fat, and/or a deficit in physical activity contributes to foggy thinking, bad decisions and

How to Maximize 24 hours and Get More Done Effortlessly

general malaise. It's tough to have a good mindset when you're tired and sluggish. It might be all in your mind, but you've got to feed it the right stuff!

Be grateful: By focusing on the good things and people in your life, you are making room for more. Putting the spotlight on only what is negative prevents you from appreciating what you have.

Abundance attracts abundance.

Mindset isn't just about saying positive things. It's about internalizing what you say to become what you believe, and interestingly, the more you perceive with an open mind, the more good things come your way.

How to Maximize 24 hours and Get More Done Effortlessly

Motivation

Staying motivated is a tough challenge for many of us, particularly when things aren't going well – sometimes we just can't see the light at the end of the tunnel. How do we keep our energy up even when we don't feel so energetic?

Motivation is a highly studied topic in the field of psychology – especially in terms of our internal and external reasons for doing what we do. External motivators include prestige, recognition, money and praise, while internally we are motivated by qualities such as feeling a sense of accomplishment, enjoying our work, personal development and reaching long term personal goals.
In short, doing our work for the external motivator of money isn't enough to sustain us. While it can certainly satisfy the very important need for financial security and buy us things, it won't keep us going on those discouraging days. Instead, we need to figure out our Big Why – what do we get up in the morning for everyday?

Everyone's Big Why is different. I am motivated by wanting to leave a legacy, give to my family, share what I know about organization and productivity with others, and write books. One of my colleagues tells me she is motivated by wanting to visit every continent, entertain her grandchildren, and have $500 in her wallet at any given time. It's not the money, she explains, but the feeling that it gives her.

When we run into those obstacles that come along, it's the Big Why we can return to again and again to keep us going. So, what's your Big Why? Try asking yourself these questions to see if you can hone in on what truly motivates you and jot down your initial responses. Remember to focus on internal motivators, because these are the ones that you can determine:

How to Maximize 24 hours and Get More Done Effortlessly

What do I truly care about? It's not likely going to be cleaning the house or running errands or buying new shoes or even sending out 15 business emails today. What matters? Knowing you've done the best you can? Expressing yourself through your work? Getting to know new people? Writing that book you've always wanted to pen? Exploring the world?

What would I go to the mat for? Is it to stop cruelty to animals? Help children in need? Ensure your children's college education? Free time? Justice? Knowing this can give you not only motivation when you need it, but potential places to donate time or money.

What gets me energized on a daily basis? You may love to make calls to potential clients, or you may rather be on a long walk outside, depending on your personality. Maybe knowing you are doing valuable work that helps others? Excitement? Brain work? Learning something new?

What or who do I need when I get discouraged? Just need to talk it out or prefer to write in a journal? Maybe just a hug from someone close will do it for you. Working out or sleeping on it?

Review your list for commonalities, print and post. Identify patterns, and write down a list of your top four to five motivators. Then post these somewhere you can look at them whenever you need them. Here's an example from the colleague I mentioned earlier:

> 'Open a new window' to the world for her grandchildren
> Travel to all seven continents (four down, three to go)
> Have $500 in wallet at all times
> Give to a charity for unwanted horses
> Make a difference in my sphere of influence

Refer to your list when you are feeling down, unmotivated, and need inspiration.

How to Maximize 24 hours and Get More Done Effortlessly

Motivation is a complicated topic. Especially when we are bombarded with the day to day stuff that comes at us from all directions, threatening to take us off task. Knowing your Big Why gives you the gift of perspective.

Motivation Tip #1: Focus...
...on your intentions and goals. Of course, first you need to set your intentions and desired outcomes by planning for what you want and how to get there. Once your intentions are stated, don't let the little setbacks, sidetracks and barriers get in your way – when you look at the long term outcome of your work or activity, you are more likely to tap your internal energy and find creative ways to keep over, around or through and stay productive. Marathon runners ALWAYS picture the finish line.

Motivation Tip #2: Think...
... small steps. Set sub-goals or benchmarks that you can reach along the way and that bring your closer to your long term intention. For example, if you are an entrepreneur introducing an information product, write down your long term intention which is likely to sell a certain number of your product. Make a step by step plan to getting there, and each step becomes an outcome of its own. Marathon runners will frequently set benchmarks, for instance, the first three miles, or halfway or to the next water station so they have personally motivated celebrations along the way.

Motivation Tip #3: Remember...
...to celebrate your progress! Give yourself a reward for each mini-goal you accomplish, like taking a walk, a break, calling a friend to share your success, whatever feels like you are acknowledging yourself. This small step, celebrate, small step, celebrate tactic helps step closer to your intentions. Marathon runners frequently celebrate their progress internally by patting themselves on the back or asking supporters to be at certain points to cheer them on.

Motivation Tip #4: Talk...

How to Maximize 24 hours and Get More Done Effortlessly

…positively. You are in control of what you say to yourself, so self talk that is negative like "I can't do this" or "this is going to be hard" can be eliminated and replaced with "I CAN do this" and "this is a challenge I know I can handle" give you a different frame of reference. Surround yourself with positive people as well – complainers, whiners, and naysayers aren't going to motivate you – in fact, they almost give you permission to stay demotivated. Marathon runners tell themselves that they have trained well, they are fit, they can do it and true champions don't allow negativity into their sphere.

Motivation Tip #5: Create…
…alternatives. Sometimes motivation is impacted by too much work, seemingly endless to-do's and lack of balance in life. Design your day to give you time for recharging with a work out, walk outdoors, meditation, yoga, kayak, run, or any other activity that pulls you out of the day to day routine and work load. Most likely your Big Why for doing what you do is not so that you can work 80 hours a week. Marathon runners don't run 26 miles every day while they are in training – they have some shorter runs, some condition runs, and they take time for self care.

How to Maximize 24 hours and Get More Done Effortlessly

*N*o person is an island

If you're in business for yourself, sometimes it's tough to stay positive on those days when things don't seem to be going well and you are working from your all- by- yourself home office. You can avert this obstacle when you hire your own coach to meet with regularly and join communities of like-minded people by attending networking events and conferences. People around you who are supportive and encouraging and who believe in you help you remember why you are doing what you're doing and just how good you are at doing it. No woman is an island, and with the right support, you can keep your mindset upbeat and creative.

A book with a "Slight Edge"
Check out Jeff Olsen's book, *The Slight Edge*, if ever you find yourself wondering when all the work you are doing to develop and grow your business is going to pay off for you. You'll find out that all the little things (and big ones, too) that don't see results right away will work for you exponentially if you maintain your positive mindset and keep at it. You'll learn how to make the right decisions on a daily basis and how to keep that positive mindset that can lead to your dreams. You can get your copy of *The Slight Edge* at any bookseller.

I didn't get anything done today
How many times have you said, "I didn't get anything done today?" Being productive isn't always about your to do list, which we all know, gets interrupted by the unexpected phone calls, drop ins, emails or myriad of other break-ins during your day. Often, when you say you didn't accomplish much, you actually did – just not what you originally planned. If you change your mindset and your statement, instead of berating yourself, you can be positive and realistic, giving yourself the credit you deserve: "Today I handled all the curve balls that came my way with grace and ease."

How to Maximize 24 hours and Get More Done Effortlessly

It's about believing you are the boss of you
You are the determinant of your destiny. Yes, true you are not in control of what comes up in your life but you ARE in control of how you handle what is handed to you. And that's where a positive mindset can make all the difference. Psychologists call it the "internal locus of control" and the "external locus of control." Those who believe the things "happen to them" and who place blame for their lives on others or on circumstances are living in external locus, closing the world of possibilities and opportunities. While it may be true that things happen, when you respond in a way that is best for and benefits you, you are controlling what you can and that's what a positive mindset is all about.

Think it, believe it, and then take action!
Just saying you want something in your life isn't enough, even in the world of the law of attraction. You'll want to be taking steps to get there. Say you want a thriving, prosperous business of your own. You can speak affirmations about it, pray for it, and even believe it -- all super positive mindset steps. But the real practice of mindset is about thinking AND doing so you are using your many strengths and talents to get to your goal.

How to Maximize 24 hours and Get More Done Effortlessly

How to get inspiration when you most need it....

Feeling inspired is a remarkable thing. Inspiration acts as a motivator, a mood lifter, a creative source and gives us that extra energy to do whatever we set out to do. Note how athletes do better when inspired by a coach or a personal event in their lives, how entrepreneurs working from home grow into six figure businesses with the right support, how productivity in corporations soars when employees and leaders are inspired in their vision and their work.

Yet what inspires you may not be what does it for me or anyone else because inspiration is an internalized factor. While you may love a certain song and find it to ratchet up your energy and creativity level, someone else might find that same song to have no meaning at all. No worries, there are a number of ways to tap into inspiration and here are several – you can choose the ones that will work best to inspire you to reach for the stars.

Sing, Sing a Song...: Whether you sing along, dance, play an instrument, or put on headphones and listen to the many nuances of the instruments and voices, music is an incredible source of inspiration. Choose songs or musical scores that have meaning for you, give yourself a half an hour and just let it rip.

Print and Post: I've been noticing lately a proliferation of inspirational quotes on Facebook, interest, and in newsletters and other on and off line posts. I'm a bit split on the subject, because some of these do catch my attention for a minute, while the rest I just scroll by. The posting of quotes has become more the norm, so I think it's easy to build immunity to them. That being said, I do think they have value. When you find one that is particularly meaningful to you, go ahead and print and post it on your screensaver or somewhere else you will see it often. Here's one of my favorites: Obstacles are what we see when we take our eyes off the goal.

How to Maximize 24 hours and Get More Done Effortlessly

A Chapter a Day: Make it a daily practice to read something inspirational or spiritual. Whether you choose to read from Deepak Chopra's latest work or something like The Slight Edge by Jeff Olsen, you can set a goal to read a chapter or few pages every morning. It is AMAZING how this kind of regular reading can set up your day to be full of creativity, inspiration and peace.

Meditate on it! Many people use meditation as a daily practice, but you can use it when you are in particular need of a 'divine download' as well. All the regular rules apply: quiet place, comfortable position, predetermined time (start with five minutes), focus on breathing, and clearing your mind. In this quiet place, you'll find strength and inspiration you didn't even know you had.

Meet up: You've heard the story again and again: sad person being encouraged by friends to go out with them and have fun, sad person says no, group says yes, person goes, feels better. It's trite, but true that our friends can lift our spirits, provided we have surrounded ourselves with positive people. Same for colleagues – often going to a planned conference or workshop that forces us to interact can open our minds and get us in touch with our creative selves and provide the inspiration to move forward.

Talk with a Mentor: There's a reason why people hire personal, life, business, productivity and accountability coaches: inspiration. Just talking with someone who knows you and what you want to accomplish can give you renewed energy and a perspective you might otherwise not see because you are too close to the problem. Your coach or mentor can often help you with those blindsides that block your productivity.

Walk it out: Treadmill, walk in the park, yoga, work out – whatever works for you. Exercise is a frequent prescription for those looking for motivation and inspiration – that's because it changes your brain chemistry and promotes improved mood and creative juices. A walk

How to Maximize 24 hours and Get More Done Effortlessly

outdoors can give you incredible perspective and inspiration as you experience the vast creativity in nature.

Sleep on it: Pay attention to your dreams. Frequently, when you dream, you are processing problems from your day, challenges and issues on your mind. Many find that solutions and ideas come to them in their dreams, giving a fresh look and helping them get unstuck, which is inspiring in and of itself!

Back to class: For me, nothing inspires like learning something new, getting those 'aha' moments, opening my mind to new ideas and thoughts. Attending workshops, taking a class, either in your field or about your avocation, will present possibilities that you've never considered, and motivate you to pursue them.

Try something new: As a writer, I know the guideline that when you are stuck in your plot or story, introduce something a little outrageous or opposite to what's expected. Same principle applies here: step out of your comfort zone and try something completely different and new. It can be anything from a hot air balloon ride, to zip lining, to setting a goal that's both exciting and a stretch.

Artwork rocks: While watching Project Runway, I took my inspiration from the contestants visit to the Guggenheim Museum of Modern Art, and their assignment to use art as a basis for their designs. We can do the same. Seeing what others have created that we might never have even conceived of can be exciting, fresh and feed our creative side.

Clearing your space: With my history as a productivity and organizational expert, I couldn't NOT mention organization as a source of inspiration. When you have a clean slate around you and inside you as well, you will find yourself move available for inspirational moments.

How to Maximize 24 hours and Get More Done Effortlessly

The actual definition of inspiration is "the process of being mentally stimulated to do or feel something, especially to do something creative". Without inspiration, our projects, programs, services are harder to accomplish and we may not reach our goals. Use these inspiration tips to feed your internal creator and to stay motivated.

Too much to do = lack of inspiration
It's difficult to stay motivated when you have too much going on – a heaping plate of to-do's, where you are trying to juggle too many tasks. The result is your energy is drained, and you become unsure where to direct the little energy remaining. You can inspire yourself to move forward when you whittle your giant to do list down to a few priorities for a certain period of time. For example, review your task list and pick the top two items that will move you forward the most. Do those first and if there is any time left, attack the next two. You'll be inspiring yourself by accomplishing what's important rather than discouraging yourself trying to do everything.
Tip: You can do anything you want to do, but you can't do everything.

Open mindedness is the key to inspiration
When we open our personal windows and doors, we become more able to listen to new ideas, ways of doing things, feedback and creative inspiration. It's so easy to close ourselves off if we are solopreneurs or working on a project alone. We come up with ideas and try to take action, but it's a bit like working in a vacuum or from an ivory tower. Without allowing the world in, we have to continually depend on only our ideas. They might be good ones, but with an open mind, you can be inspired to make them better.

The Internet is your inspirational friend
While sometimes the Internet can be a time drainer, when it comes to inspiration, it is a gift. Really. It takes just a few minutes to find an inspirational quote or quotes, a video that motivates, or an article that gets you back in the saddle. Try famousquotes.com where I found: "Without inspiration the best powers of the mind remain

How to Maximize 24 hours and Get More Done Effortlessly

dormant, there is a fuel in us which needs to be ignited with sparks." *(Johann Gottfried Von Herder)*. For videos, I love ted.com, from which you can choose short videos on a variety of topics, including inspiration! For inspirational articles, I just do a search and find one. Take about 15 minutes a day to find your quotes, video or article and you'll find getting inspired is easier.

Let the inspiration in!
Ever have those days when inspiration just hits and you are off and running on your task or project? Maybe you are doing marketing writing and you can't type on the keyboard fast enough to keep up with your ideas. Or you're organizing a room and you get a brilliant idea. Problem is that inspiration seems to come and go, as there are other days where you'd rather walk on glass than do that marketing writing or your room organization project is just picking something up and moving it somewhere else. You do have some input on inspiring yourself and you can do it more easily than you think. Try reading, consulting, even dancing around the room. Once you let in more, more inspiration arrives with it!

The Inspiration Mindset Quiz
How many times a week do you wake up and think about all the things you have to do today and how busy you will be and how you don't have enough time?

How many days a week are you operating in full out stress mode?

How many times this week have you delayed starting or working on a project?

If you answered more than once to any of the above questions, your mindset is negatively impacting your inspiration for your work or project. Try this: tell yourself that you only work in a stress free environment, or that you know how to spend time wisely, or that you have some great ideas for that project and can't wait to get

How to Maximize 24 hours and Get More Done Effortlessly

started. Print and post this wisdom on your computer or board to remember that you can stay inspired simply by how you think!

How to Maximize 24 hours and Get More Done Effortlessly

Working through uncertainty

One of the major reasons we lose momentum when it comes to reaching our goals is the feeling of uncertainty:

Can I do it?

Am I ready to do what it takes?

What if my efforts aren't good enough?

Do I really know what I am doing?

How do I know if the outcome will be what I want?

Keeping on track to reaching our goals is part expertise, part patience, part making the effort and part just plain faith in ourselves and our abilities. When you experience uncertainty, take a moment to make a short list that includes your Big Why – the purpose of your goals, the strengths and support you have to help you get there, and what you will need to make it happen. You'll get perspective and confidence.

When problems come to town...

Whether you are starting a business, reorganizing your basement or training a new puppy, you can count on one thing: problems will arise to try to take you off course from your goals. But it's not the problems that are the problem: it's how you view them. Every single time you resolve a new issue that gets in the way of your ultimate objective you are getting closer to reaching it. Expect problems – also expect you know what to do to overcome them. Give yourself a time cushion, make contingency plans, and be creative about integrating your solutions.

How to Maximize 24 hours and Get More Done Effortlessly

Keep your vision front and center

Use a vision board, screen saver, montage, collage, or self-designed document to keep your long term vision for your life, business or home always visible (I have a super vision board kit my clients use for this purpose). When you are uncertain, down, facing obstacles or just plain tired, your vision can pull you through. Vision boards (or other formats) include visual representations of how want your life to be, reinforcing what you are working toward. For example, if traveling is big in your life, include photos of places you'd like to go; if giving back is a Big Why for your business, include logos of organizations to which you want to give contributions. Add to your board when you find more images or words. Then keep it front and center in your work area so you remain inspired.

A few words about inspiration and uncertainty
"I find inspiration almost everywhere! I am a really positive and creative person, so getting and staying inspired isn't difficult for me. One of the things that particularly helps me is variety in every form. I like to mix it up, whether it is the type of exercise I do, the type of business projects I am working on, or the type of food I am eating. Variety for me is the spice of life (and business!) and keeps me engaged, interested, challenged and helps me to avoid getting bored. I work through uncertainty by doing a "Brain Dump" so that I can get some clarity on all of the pieces involved, and plan ahead to the extent that I can. I am a big believer in writing things down to work through them. I have been keeping a journal since I am 8 years old, and that has helped me work through many periods of uncertainty. But I think what is most important for me is not working through uncertainty, but rather embracing it."
~~ Lisa Montanaro, Productivity Consultant, Success Coach, Business Strategist, Speaker, Author

Do something toward your goals every day, no matter how big or small. If you drift away or make mistakes or fail in some effort,

How to Maximize 24 hours and Get More Done Effortlessly

compassionately put yourself back on track. It's tough to "pick you up, wipe yourself off and start all over again" but it's part of the journey.

Create a workable timeline

I can tell myself I will get my major new business program done soon OR I can set up a schedule including each step and outcome that also lists my target dates. Then I can send that plan to a coach or trusted colleague so he or she can help me stay on track. Many of my clients have goals that they've had for years before working with me and the single most component that was lacking was a timetable, a deadline, a completion target. Someday, next month, next year, and when I am finished with (fill in the blank) isn't going to cut it. If you are thinking about it, if you have set it as a goal, then now is the right time to make it real. Outline a timetable for accomplishing milestones and stick to it.

"When I don't resist it, but let uncertainty just be there, with no judgment and not a ton of power over me, I can see that it is a normal part of life, and will eventually dissipate. Everything changes eventually... even uncertainty!"

~~Lisa Montanaro, Productivity Consultant, Success Coach, Business Strategist, Speaker, Author

How to Maximize 24 hours and Get More Done Effortlessly

Time Management

Email Blues

My best friend's husband reported rather proudly that he had over 350 UNREAD e-mails in his in bin.

"How do you possibly know what's in there?" I ask him, because my organizational mind can't wrap my head around his reported number. "What if there is something super important in there and you missed it?"

He finally confesses that he has missed a few rather important things, like a bill, and a message from his sister, and a client request, adding that he is slowly going through each e-mail to whittle it down, but they keep coming in faster than he can get through them.

So I asked Cena Block, Mompreneur Business Strategist, how she handles her email

"I've struggled with email in the past - especially when I used it as a task list. I've learned the hard way that to be more productive with my time, I have needed to create repeatable systems that work every time I use them."

There are people who never empty their e-mail in bin, and they can manage it quite well, and then there are others who over file to the point of exhaustion. It all depends on what works for you, but (not surprisingly), I tend to go a little more toward the organized side of this continuum.

How to Maximize 24 hours and Get More Done Effortlessly

It turns out that e-mail management is a topic all its own, and so I set my buzzing mind and a little research work to it and came up with a ton of ideas to help you manage your e-mail instead of the other way around.

Here's my recommendation: If you are employed or own your own business it is critical to **have two separate e-mail accounts,** one for personal messages and one for business. This helps you keep the client e-mails separate from your sister's recipes or your friend's jokes. It's a method of establishing separate files and it saves you from combing through personal stuff to find important business messages.

Next, **use an e-mail system that allows you to file and organize** within the system. For instance, g-mail allows for filing, archiving, labeling and marking important messages for action among many options.

Check your e-mail only twice daily, once in the morning and once in the afternoon. Set aside time for checking and responding, and then discipline yourself to the assigned times. Otherwise, you will end up in e-mail hell, where you constantly are checking your e-mail, over and over again, allowing little time to be productive in any other way. There is very little that can't wait for your twice a day log ins.

When you review e-mail, **use the classic paper management rule**: Read it, then either DELETE, SAVE IN A FILE FOR REFERENCE or ACT ON IT. Leaving items in your e-mail that you don't need make for a crowded and confusing inbox. Your goal is to get your e-mails down ten or less every time you do your twice daily check in.

Use the filing function of your e-mail for items you may want to reference in the near future. You can also use it to create special, color coded files for data that is needed for that report you are

How to Maximize 24 hours and Get More Done Effortlessly

currently creating or that product you are promoting. E-mail filing works just like paper filing, so be sure to create file names that make sense!

Be ruthless with your DELETE key. If you have read it, responded or acted, then delete it. You can judge if you'll ever need this message in the future for any reason. If on a scale of 1-10, you judge this is a 1-3 level document (unlikely to need ever again), do the delete. For 4-6 documents, you can archive them just in case. But for 7-10 documents, immediately place them in a file to get them out of your in bin.

"Although my goal is email zero, I rarely make it there. I typically received approximately 300 emails daily - with about 5-10% requiring some type of action from me. That means anywhere from 15 to 30 tasks are added to my daily tasks. This is a big reason that I build 1 day a week in for business administration. It's a necessary part of my business model. When I go on vacation, or know that I will be out of the office for extended periods of time- I sweep everything out of my inbox into a dated folder. In the case that I need to find it - it will be there, but most often, it's not necessary. On days that I am not working my system - I am not as consistent, nor efficient with my time... and have dropped out on details (which is embarrassing...), so I try to stick with what works for me. Everyone's system is different. The key for email efficiency is to take advantage of the powerful tool that it is, and stop using it as a task list."
~~ Cena Block, Mompreneur Business Strategist

Fly the flag
Try using the e-mail flags to help you categorize your incomings or mark them for action. These flags, or variations, depending on your e-mail carrier, will help remind you to follow up, forward, take action, and set automatic due dates so that you even get a reminder.

How to Maximize 24 hours and Get More Done Effortlessly

Display the colors, tags or labels
Many e-mail providers offer a color coding system, to help you either identify by category or assign to a category. For example, for a particular client named Jones, you can assign a color code to the Jones project and use that color for all e-mails related to it. You can do this with tags or labels as well, whereby you assign a tag or label to e-mails that require some action so you can easily recognize what it's about. It looks something like this:

```
My Webinar      Webinar Presentation as of 5-20-12.pptx - Looks
My Webinar      Need Orginal Art Work for the attached - Hi Deb,
Business Coaches   WOW! FREE biz and marketing services. Ha
Business Coaches   {Soul Art Studio} I am creating something nu
IAWBC           Mary Wolfburg-Hlavacek replied to the discussion "qu
STARS PROGRAM   [Stars] IMPORTANT - Your weekly call sch
```

Archive your e-mails
G-mail, as an example, gives you plenty of space to save e-mails through the archive function. This is a great place to send your e-mails if you aren't sure you will need them again, or if you want or need to have long term records. For example, if you remember that Aunt Mary sent you Uncle Mark's favorite color but you don't remember what it is, you can search your archive for her name or e-mail address and find it. If you and your client are trying to recall something you collaborated on a year ago, again, you can go back and do a search.

Filter your e-mails
You can actually filter e-mails so that they are automatically tagged based on the sender, subject line or key words when they come into your in-box. For example, if you have set up an e-mail group or you have made an offer to prospective clients that requires their response to an e-mail you send, you can arrange that all e-mails coming in from the group or the clients get automatically tagged accordingly. Many e-mail carriers offer this option. For example, in g-mail, click

How to Maximize 24 hours and Get More Done Effortlessly

on an e-mail you want to filter in the future. Go to the More in the google mail task bar, and you will find "filter" in the dropdown.

Get rid of the junk
When you check in with your e-mail account, before opening any mail, quickly scan your new mail subject lines and sender ID so you can delete all the e-mails you know you don't want today. Mark them for deletion and once you have finished perusing delete all these unwanted or unnecessary items from your in bin. Then you can go through and read the e-mails you want without being distracted by the ones you don't want. Experts estimate anywhere between 50 and 75% of our in bin is unwanted, especially if we don't "unsubscribe" to the sources from whom we no longer wish to receive e-mails.

Get your ".doc's" in order
If you ever have trouble staying organized (with anything), the same might be true with the countless computer files you may be juggling. I've heard tell of people being unable to find computer stored information because it's been filed in obscure or arbitrary folders.

It's easy to just press "save" and just know that your file is saved, somewhere, figuring you'll remember how to find it. But if you've ever looked for a file by opening document after document only to find everything but what you're looking for until you get to document 63, now's the time to get your files in order.

Here are some tips on getting a proper system in place so you can easily find your .docs and other files in a jif.

Your computer filing plan takes time, but saves MORE time later.

How to Maximize 24 hours and Get More Done Effortlessly

Step 1. Folders rock!
Use online folders for your word, PowerPoint, excel, and pdf files. Use folder names that will still make sense to you a year from today, for example use "Business Receipts 20XX" instead of "Stuff for taxes". You are less likely to misfile using succinct and clear folder names. If you are running your own business, be sure to keep separate business and personal folders so you can easily find your client information without wading through all the recipes you've been saving.

Step 2. Create Folders Within Folders
Too many folders can be just like having too many files. Creating sub-folders keeps the list of folders manageable, but still gives you sub-sets when you need them (like when you actually click on them). These folders are quickly accessible, yet invisible. They show up only when they're needed. So in your Personal folder, create a sub folder called Recipes. Or, in your Business folder, a subfolder called Ideas.

Step 3. Repeat as Necessary
Do this process over again as needed. Categorize at lower and lower levels until each document is truly in the right, logical place.

How do I know if I've gone too far?
If a folder contains only one document, or items in a directory share nothing in common with each other, then you've mis- or over-categorized.

If you are starting your own personal collection of documents, quit and start an antique spoon collection instead as it will likely have more value. Save to your newly organized file folders only what you absolutely need. It's a bit like saving every piece of paper because you might need it someday, only to be buried in useless stacks later.

How to Maximize 24 hours and Get More Done Effortlessly

Bonus Tip:
"When I'm working at top productivity, I handle email well by following these rules.

1. I don't look at email first thing. I typically wait until after I've completed the top priority task (or two for the day) on my list.

2. When it's email time, I scan my entire inbox of email for things that require my follow up action, flag them in email and immediately add any action items to my to do list.

3. If the email requires action or input from someone else, I move the email file to a pending folder.

4. I have sub folders where I store important emails, but have found this step unnecessary as searching capabilities have become more robust.

5. During downtime once every two weeks or so I will sweep my email, tag junk mail, unsubscribe where I can, and delete my trash.

6. The best practice I have is to move things out of email immediately onto my task list when they require follow up action. When I don't things tend to fall through the cracks.

7. I manage my business and virtual teams using an online cloud-based team tool - Asana. It saves SO much time back and forth and has drastically increased my teams ability to efficiently communicate and share information.

8. My challenge now is managing the tasks that come in through social media... Often things happen with clients, colleagues and collaborators via the social media platforms - and if I neglect my 'tried-and-true system', I drop out those details."

~~ Cena Block, Mompreneur Business Strategist

How to Maximize 24 hours and Get More Done Effortlessly

Knowing When to Let Go

There are two sides of the "I Feel Overwhelmed" coin:

Side One – You really do have too much stuff to do. Only *you* can thin the herd and know what things on the list can be dropped. Here's something to consider: some of the things that we think are un-droppable really aren't. We get to decide and sometimes there's going to be "to do's" that can get crossed out or moved to a "maybe, someday" list.

I recently asked one of my colleagues what they do when they have too much on their plate

"I like to go for a walk--preferably down by the marina. It's a powerful combination with the calming influence of water for unblocking creativity and the productivity boost of exercise. If I can't go for a walk, I take calming breaths. The next thing is to do a brain dump, usually by a mind map, to get the clutter of thoughts out of my head. This creates an overview of all the projects competing for my attention."
~~ Nicole Chamblin, *MA, CPO®*, of Visions Productivity Solutions

Side Two – You feel like you're the one who has to do everything (when in fact, this isn't actually true).

Side Two is a whole lot easier to deal with. Recently, I talked with a friend who took charge of a proposal involving an enormous event planning project. Feeling that the responsibility to pull-it-off was all on her, she was more than a little stressed. She explained that the event had many components that needed to be 'perfect', and she had other projects to work on as well. What to do?

How to Maximize 24 hours and Get More Done Effortlessly

Firm believer in delegation that I am, I helped her divide up responsibilities and research among her friends and assistant. By the same afternoon she has the information she needed for the proposal.

What she thought would take days, took only a half a day, and her stress went from sky high to knee high.

You can treat the "I have to do it all myself because no one does it the way I would do it" syndrome when you concentrate on these few key tips on delegating that bring you surprising freedom, time and considerably less stress!

Steer clear of perfectionism when it isn't needed. Most things don't have to be perfect, they just have to be. That means someone else can do them besides you.

There is always **more than one way to get things done**, and while your delegate might not do it your way, if the results are equal or better, isn't that what really counts?

Think of yourself as a manager. You know what needs to get done, and how. Break the job down into smaller tasks and do a quick brainstorm on who might be able to take care of some of the smaller pieces of the puzzle. Your virtual assistant? Your partner? A temp? Be creative....

Delegation doesn't mean abdication. You are still in charge. You can set the tone, the goals and the path. Just let someone else help with the driving.

Give the right amount of direction. Some of those you choose to delegate to will need more instructions than others. Try to give freedom for people to do it their way when you can, as they will be more motivated if they have some latitude and responsibility. Don't micromanage, but be available to answer questions.

How to Maximize 24 hours and Get More Done Effortlessly

If it's scary to let go, **try it with just one thing**. Just one, then add another, and another, and pretty soon you will get hooked on the power of delegation.

And here's a super cool bonus: delegation often strengthens professional (or even personal) relationships because it also empowers and validates the people you are working with.

Letting go can be an amazingly scary and exciting experience. The truth is, there are plenty of people who can do things as well as you (and, yes, maybe even better!), if you give them the chance, and you will end up being more productive in the long run.

How to Maximize 24 hours and Get More Done Effortlessly

Hourglass and Internet

It happens all the time. You sit down in front of a screen to complete a task. You open a browser to "check" something real quick. You follow a few links, then close the browser to get back to work—only to be looking at a still-empty screen. Not to mention the hour that just passed.

But I did so much, you say, *how can I have nothing to show for it?*

Internet distractions create problems for businesses, employees, those who work from home, students and just about everyone employees alike. In fact, there are those who actually become addicted, falling victim to that net-full of information and activities. Among the culprits (and these are just a few) are: your e-mail in bin, Facebook, Wikipedia, blogsites, games, YouTube, MySpace, news and travel sites — Google in general.

It is so very easy to get sidetracked. Following the e-mail trail starts this off course journey. You know the drill. You are working on a task and realize that you need some information in your e-mail files or a response from someone you e-mailed. You open your e-mail looking for just this one piece of information and ... distraction attack!

Precious minutes....
Time is a commodity, like money, with one difference - we can't get a time raise or a second job to make more time. That makes it ever more important that we "spend" our time carefully. Wasted time is any time that goes by that hasn't been used to serve us, and this is often caused by the willful donation of our minutes to unworthy causes OR the mysterious evaporation of these minutes all together as is the case when we allow the Internet to steal our precious minutes.

How to Maximize 24 hours and Get More Done Effortlessly

Time also gets wasted in the act of *RE*-focusing. Not only do we waste time during distractions, but the time it takes to re-acquaint ourselves with the original task also becomes poorly spent time, lost forever.

Here are some quick tips to help you avoid Internet temptations.....
Wear a shield: Boundaries (like bowling with bumpers) allow us to head in the direction we want, while gently keeping us on course. If you *really do* need to order those shoes (something you have predetermined), order them and then sign-off. Shopping is the culprit here, not the website.

Ban link chasing: If you actually need to look something up on Wikipedia, do so—but don't go diving down rabbit holes of 'research' (unless research is your true job). You'll find that in most cases chasing links becomes another means of avoidance of the work at hand.

Cultivate mindfulness: Sometimes we wander off to a distracting site without even realizing it, a little like eating the whole bag of cookies before we know they are gone. Grab a kitchen timer and set it for ten minutes. When it goes off, ask yourself, *what am I doing right now, at this moment?* There are an array of pleasant sounds (meditation bells, nature noises, etc.) for both phones and computers. Timer apps are common and very available too.

Out of sight, out of mind: Avoid leaving websites open if they're on your blacklist. Check sites, (emails, etc.) intentionally, and for a specific message or purpose. Leaving tempting sites open only invites trouble. It's a bit like putting five open candy bars in front of you and trying to deny yourself. Torture!

Be the boss of your time: If it's four o'clock, decide you want to have that proposal done by five. Does opening a new browser page for no really good reason at 4:37 help the cause? Probably not.

How to Maximize 24 hours and Get More Done Effortlessly

Work in bursts Stay off the web and away from the phone for short periods of time. Allot a certain period of time each day for checking e-mail or returning phone calls.

Take baby steps If you're someone who checks your email every other minute, try starting by setting a time for fifteen minutes, during which time you vow not to check your in bin. Then slowly move the time to bigger and bigger chunks. No need to go Cold Turkey.

Make an Oath Say *I will do this task, without chasing distractions, for the next 30 minutes*. A half hour may not seem like a lot, but several bursts of uninterrupted productivity like this may prove very lucrative overall.

Get a little help from.....
...software! For some of us, a little help might be just the ticket. There are software and programming solutions to rescue us:

Freedom – (available for Mac and PC) is a relatively inexpensive program that locks you out of the Internet for as long as you tell it to.

Self Control – (Mac only) is more invasive but allows you more specific control. You pick the sites or programs on your blacklist; *Self Control* completely disables access to them for a length of time determined by you. Be careful, this is an ABSOLUTE LOCKOUT. Turning off your computer, re-booting, even uninstalling the program will do nothing to bring back those sites. You HAVE to wait until the time is up to regain access to your favorite distractions.

In the big picture, you are the only one who gets to decide how to spend your time. Is it going to be two hours of being zoned out in Farmville or two hours of .... something better?

How to Maximize 24 hours and Get More Done Effortlessly

Know thy enemy Some of us react to certain websites as if they were some sort of cyber drug. We can't seem to say no, we stay on them longer than we intended—even when they cause us trouble.

We waste precious minutes of our lives, sometimes even losing money over it rite but true: the first step is recognizing your problem. Ask yourself, do I really want my tombstone to read "She was a really great Bejeweled Blitz player?" The powerful Distraction Vortex of the Internet is real. Seek help if you are in too deep.

Establish time zones Besides robbing us of time, Internet distractions also break our concentration. More productivity is lost *RE*-focusing than we think. Trying to put in several hours without being pulled away by diversions can be hard, but working un-interrupted is important (and often essential). It's easier to work for an interruption-free 30 minute block so time yourself and start there.

Know your limitations Why tempt temptation? You know certain programs and websites will suck you in every time. Staying logged-in is like a constant invitation. Programs minimized on a task bar are just a click away (and that much easier to get wrapped up in). Don't leave distracting browser pages open. Close programs that you know you don't really want to be using during productive time.

Stick to your guns If you must go to a "*danger* site", stick to the point and be specific about your purpose. Browsing, "window" shopping and surfing (chasing those shiny links that look *oh so enticing*) are usually what get us into trouble. Decide ahead of time exactly what you want or what you're going for. Get in -- and get out.

What's important to you? Getting a project complete? Being with your children or partner? Cooking a fabulous meal? Building your business? Creating a masterpiece? Whatever it is, surfing the net isn't going to get you there. Post a list of your priorities so you can

How to Maximize 24 hours and Get More Done Effortlessly

easily remind yourself every time you are online of exactly what is important to you. Then ask how the task you are doing online is helping (or not helping) you reach your goals.

How to Maximize 24 hours and Get More Done Effortlessly

*S*tick to your goals when everything is important

We all do it—try to juggle too many things at the same time, leaving no time for the unexpected. Or worse, we schedule two things at the same time. There comes a point when we get tired of saying "I'm so sorry, I must have double-booked," or "I hate being late, it won't happen again". We realize we have to do something... but what?

When we take on too much we feel stressed and MAXed-out. We try to cut things out, but *everything* seems important. Time management strategies can help, but many of us **DO** actually take on more than we can handle. We fill our plate to the point of over-flowing, and when one more thing comes our way, we feel like the whole world is going to collapse.

Undue stress and pressure caused by over-doing and over-booking can lead to:

- burnout
- loss of productivity
- depression
- car accidents
- trouble sleeping
- overeating
- substance abuse
- accidental injuries

On top of that, if our lives are overbooked, we probably aren't taking care of ourselves (mentally, emotionally, and spiritually).

Also important: are we feeding the relationships that are most important in our lives?

Start by getting it straight
If you find that you are in fact over-scheduling and over-committing yourself and need more than just time management skills, here are some things to consider:

How to Maximize 24 hours and Get More Done Effortlessly

Find out what's what by doing a quick inventory of what's important. Where are you spending your time? What things are really important to you? Time is like a commodity that we spend.

What are you buying with your time and is it making you crazy or content?

Structure Counts: Make a bottom line and try not to break it. For example, leave your desk or work at a predetermined time every day and don't allow anyone, including you, to step over your line.

Taking care of your schedule is taking care of yourself. You won't be able to perform your best if you are stressed and overwhelmed and only you can set the rules.

Get Real by being realistic about what's possible and what's not. Some of us are overly ambitious and idealistic about what we can accomplish in a given day. Try to focus on one major item and two minor ones each day, period. When you add more than five things on today's to do list, plus your appointments and calls, you are setting yourself up to be exhausted and not meet your goals.

Protect your time and your well-being. Establish clear boundaries around your time. For instance, accepting interruptions via texts and phone calls while you are working on a project means that you are not in charge of your time. It means that everyone else is the boss of you.

When you've whittled everything down to the essentials, try these strategies for maximizing your newly boundary, structured, real scheduled time:

Let calls go to voicemail.
Make calls in batches.

How to Maximize 24 hours and Get More Done Effortlessly

Prep what you will need before diving into a string of meetings/errands/appointments and build that prep time into your schedule

How do I know if I'm overbooking or just being productive?
So often, small, reasonable things pop up in our day-to-day activities. If we've overbooked our day, these normal things can throw us for a loop. For this we need what I call *Wise Scheduling*.

Anticipate the "X Factor": You need time built-in for unexpected events or 'emergencies', otherwise these things can over drain even the best-intentioned system.

Build buffers into your schedule by:

Carving out time for un-anticipated calls or meetings, then if nothing unexpected does come up, use this time to do short, personal or organization tasks.

Giving yourself a fifteen minute break between meetings/appointments so you don't have to stress if a meeting goes over a few minutes. Use the break to make notes on your meeting or to get up and stretch.

Giving yourself adequate time to do offsite errands or appointments, so you don't end up with road rage or being late!

I'm still taking on too much!
Learn to avoid the martyr syndrome by saying "NO" or "Not Now". Try these statements on and see which works best for you.

~Sorry, I'm totally booked right now. I'd love to work with you and have an opening to talk about it in (two weeks). (There's no shame in having a full schedule!)

How to Maximize 24 hours and Get More Done Effortlessly

~I'd really like to help you on this, but I don't have enough time in my schedule to do the great job you deserve. Can we revisit this next week?

~I might not be the best person for the job but I can recommend someone else that would be good at it.
~No, that just doesn't fit into my schedule right now.

Saying no can be difficult, whether it's personal or professional, because we want everyone to like us and because we don't want to turn down possible opportunities. But remember, while we can do anything we want to do, we cannot do everything. There's more value in acting as a human being instead of a human doing.

Too much good stuff can be a bad thing Lack of sleep, deteriorating health, depression, compulsive habits—sounds like the symptoms of some horrible syndrome, right? What if you were the cause of some of these things in your own life? Unnecessary stress and constantly feeling overwhelmed can contribute to all of these things. A lesson in how to stop over-booking may alleviate a lot more than you think.

Take that! ('Cause I don't want it) Learning to let go of things can be hard. Not taking them on in the first place can be easier. An exercise in learning how to say *NO* to new things we really don't have time for can go a long way toward securing a contented life.

There's power in numbers! Returning emails and calls in batches, as well as grouping other similar tasks, can make for a huge step towards *Wise Scheduling*. Establishing time zones for these 'every day' jobs is also a much needed practice for many.

Don't pick yourself last No one likes to get picked last. So why put yourself at the bottom of the list when it comes to time, energy and fulfillment? Taking care of yourself is an investment; give yourself

How to Maximize 24 hours and Get More Done Effortlessly

the gift of health and ease. On the productivity side, self-care will actually pay off with incredible dividends.

Expect the unexpected Life is full of "X- Factors". Failing to admit this can drive a person insane. Leave yourself some room in your schedule **each day**, and watch as the "little stuff" seems to find its way off your list.

Give yourself a break Treating everyone well except yourself might not be serving the big picture. (Think airplane oxygen masks — you have to take care of yourself first!) Many of us need to actually designate specific time in our planners and calendars for workouts, naps and recreation. Never underestimate the importance of time needed for decompressing after (or even during) a long or stressful day.

Connected day and night via laptops, cell phones, iPads and exponentially increasing technology, it's tough to draw lines between personal and professional lives so that both get the attention they need. Managers expect employees to be continuously available, employees call their boss at home with problems, and entrepreneurs who work at home face extra challenges when it comes to work-life balance.

Creativity and productivity enhancement soar when you have a respite from work in whatever form you take it. Yet by checking business e-mail at home, taking work-related calls during vacation, or doing professional projects on the laptop during supposed down time, the opportunity for re-energizing is lost.

How to Maximize 24 hours and Get More Done Effortlessly

Staying Organized

Paper Filing

How does Barbara Hemphill 'tame the paper tiger?'

"Clutter is postponed decisions®. There are only three decisions you can make about any piece of paper:

File - For future reference (with a File Index so you can find it again — or scan it and store electronically)

Act - What specifically do you need to do? By when? Are you the best person to do it?

Toss - recycle or shred"

~~Barbara Hemphill, Founder, Productive Environment Institute

We've all had that moment… much like the Wild West showdown when we attempt to stare down a desk or tabletop covered in paper. Notes, bills, unopened mail, kids school papers, assignments, contracts. It's the good, bad and the ugly -- without the good.

Attacking such a monstrosity may seem like it will take even more time than it's worth (or than we're willing to give). But when we think of the swirling stress and the time wasted, we know deep down inside that we aren't going to win the showdown unless we make the first move. Because this isn't going to end in a draw and there's only going to be one winner.

How to Maximize 24 hours and Get More Done Effortlessly

Most of us hold onto paper because we're worried we'll forget what's on it, so we leave it out as a reminder or to file later, or refer to it if we need it or maybe because we just don't know what else to do with it.

That's where I come in, the organization and productivity sheriff, here to help you start **a system and stick to it**, then watch the paper vanish, as you feel a sense of empowerment rising up from within.

How to shoot down the paper
Try to **go paper-less** (bills, newsletters, etc.) if given the option online by your provider.

Eliminate junk mail You can write to the following address (ask them to take you off their "direct mailing" list): Mail Preference Service, Direct Marketing Association P.O. Box 9008, Farmingdale, NY 11735-9008

Use technology. Mini-scanners are a combination of a copy machine and a magic wand. Hand-held and barely longer than a ruler, you run one over a page or image to record it digitally, then save it to your appropriate computer file. Paper disappears!

Try software like *Highrise*, a subscription service that can help you stay organized. Think of it as a personal, electronic secretary. It has an abundance of features such as keeping meeting notes, documents and contracts, tracking proposals and deals, setting reminders and keeping track of conversations and dates. You can use *Highrise* to **share** just about anything with selected co-workers. *Highrise* will even connect with email and the Internet, and has apps for Android or iPhones.

Evernote is a free program designed to help you eliminate paper. You can use it to save or share snippets from documents, web pages, articles, photos—even audio files.

How to Maximize 24 hours and Get More Done Effortlessly

"Research shows that 80% of the paper you keep, you never use! So, how do you decide what you really need to keep? Ask the question, "What's the worst possible thing that would happen if I didn't have this piece of paper?" If you can live with your answer, toss, recycle or shred!"

~~ Barbara Hemphill, Founder, Productive Environment Institute

If you must keep the paper...

You can think of organizing paper in terms of **4 categories: Now, Later** and **Always** and **Never.**

There are a few supplies you should have handy (usually you have these things but haven't been using them to their best potential.....
Small filing cabinet
Accordion file (or multiples, for different purposes)
3 Ring Binder (s) – and plastic sheets, dividers (just like in school)

Now, quickly triage your paper pile using these **4 Categories**:

The Never File -- something you just aren't going to need ever or if on the 1% chance you might use it in the next five years, you could look it up online. So stuff like empty envelopes, advertisements, promotions, flyers. You know where this file goes: the circular file.

The Always File – something that will always be with you. Very important, long-term-use documents (passports, medical records, policies, contracts, tax information etc...) that do not require immediate action and are not part of a To-Do list.

The Later File – things you don't want to forget about, that you'd ideally like to tackle in the near future (like, this week) but not necessarily today.

How to Maximize 24 hours and Get More Done Effortlessly

The NOW File – Today's To-Do List. Actions that need to be addressed in the next day or so. *Action Tip:* Get a desk folder-holder and use simple manila folders for the NOW File and the Later File—that way they're out and accessible, but not an eyesore.

Use a Kill Plan to keep Short Term files from becoming a Long Term files (a.k.a. "pile-up").
The KEY to having a successful Kill Plan is to design a set of rules that you ruthlessly follow in order to make yourself throw things out. Everyone's will look different, but try using these methods of execution once you have one.

Start at the back (the older stuff) and work forward. It is easier to make decisions this way. This also builds confidence and momentum.

Set a timer for 30-60 seconds. You can do almost anything for a minute! Ruthlessly eliminate as much as possible during the set time. Doing this a few times will thin the herd by half, faster than you think.

Eliminate 1 item a month/week/day, *or*… 1 item every time you dip into that file, *or*… 1 item every time you add a new file/item.

Again, delete from the back (oldest) as you add to the front.

Eliminate some of your paper load before...
... it ever gets to your table/desk. Try these new habits/behaviors:

Throw away non-essentials - Do your sorting, sifting and mail-opening by the trash. Get rid of return envelopes, advertisements, etc.

Do *it* or file *it* right away whenever possible - respond to invitations, tack dates to the fridge or mark something on a calendar

How to Maximize 24 hours and Get More Done Effortlessly

immediately if it's notice, announcement or something that doesn't require any thought or complex action.

Eliminate whole pieces of paper - Pair-down or clip important parts of things. Then put your clippings in an envelope or folder (to be filed IMMEDIATLEY!). Get rid of the rest.

Replace large papers or piles with Post-It notes – write tasks as a Catch Phrase on a small note. Stick these to a regular piece of paper. File or stow the original documents or stacks so they're out of your space. This new To-Do sheet will keep you from forgetting. The entire mass can usually be reduced to one, 8" x 11" piece of paper. Whether you are a paper hoarder, a paper thrower, a paper piler, or a paper delayer, you can use these tips above so you don't have to deal with a show down ever again.

Go Lean Get rid of paper documents, reminders, notes and other files by using computer programs and phone apps that work like a personal secretary or cork board on steroids. Got something already on paper that you REALLY can't stand to lose? Scan it, save it, and forget about it (for the time being, anyway).

Be trashy! No, really. Hangout by the trash when you go through your mail and when you're sorting through documents, paperwork, etc. Instantly get rid of all the "filler" (advertisements, return envelopes… junk) before it ever hits the clutter zone.

All Systems GO! You may be staring at something that's in your way, but that you're afraid you are going to need SOON, LATER, or FOREVER. Regardless, you have to have a *system* for how you will put these things to rest. One word for you: Priorities! Prioritize using the NOW, NEVER, MAYBE SOMEDAY and KEEP system and you'll be able to convert an entire desktop full of paper confusion into a single piece of 8X11 paper.

How to Maximize 24 hours and Get More Done Effortlessly

Get your GREEN on. Nature loves a paper-less work space as much as you do. Don't forget the basics of avoiding paper piles before they ever exist. Un-subscribe from Master Junk Mail lists, and go paperless with bills and notifications whenever possible.

Good riddance! It feels good to chip away at the growing paper landfill that may be "taking over" your space. If you haven't been successful with getting rid of old paperwork in the past, try some truly manageable strategies for *attacking the stack*. No Spring Cleaning here, just a simple method for letting go of a few things here-and-there, that translates into a lot less paper debris sooner than you think.

How to Maximize 24 hours and Get More Done Effortlessly

What's getting in YOUR way?

Organization – there are workshops, books, seminars, conferences, postings, and lectures on the topic galore! You would think the topic would be old by now, but thankfully for me, an organization and productivity expert, it's just as hot as ever.

That's because organization can make the difference as described here:

Organization benefits	Disorganization costs
Successful business	Doing OK or worse business
Feeling of peace and calm	Constantly panicked or frantic
Reaching goals	Straying off goal
Working responsibly	Things falling through the big crevices
Being on top of your game	Playing catch up
Managing your business	Overwhelmed
Ease of everything easily found	Searching for hours for your keys
Heading somewhere	Heading nowhere
Easier to take what life presents…	Closing off to life experience

Organized people have an easier day to day life! Of course I have a number of strategies and tips on organization, and you can check my blog and website for a plethora of postings on the topic.

Right now, though, I want to focus on the obstacles to organizing and how to overcome them so you can experience the benefits of an organized life and business.

Challenge #1: I don't have the time. This is likely happening because you're letting time and circumstance be your boss instead of the other way around. Time management is a form of organization – you do have time – if you choose to use it wisely.

How to Maximize 24 hours and Get More Done Effortlessly

From another standpoint, organized people DO have time because of the very fact they are organized. The return on investment of time into a smooth and organized system is usually 200% -or more. That means for every hour you spend on organizing, you get two hours to do what you love to do.

Challenge #2: I don't know where to start. You are in overwhelmed. Overwhelm often leads to inertia, and not knowing where to start is a manifestation of that inertia. Like any other project, take it in small steps. If it's your basement, start with one corner only. If it's your business projects, start with one project at a time. Or try allowing yourself 1 hour per day to devote to organization. Yet another option is to get professional help – another pair of eyes, especially organized ones, can help you see the light at the end of your disorganization tunnel.

Challenge #3: I'm just not an organized person and I'm fine with that. That's cool. I don't believe in forcing people to organize their personal or business lives and environments. I do like to point out the opening list in this chapter and ask on which side you would rather be. And, I also advise asking yourself these questions:

How is my lack of organization affecting the quality of my life, the amount of time for me, and/or the income of my business?

How is my lack of organization affecting the quality of other people's lives?

If money and time were no object, would I choose to be organized?

Challenge #4: I start, but never stick to my organization plan. Congrats on starting! Something is getting in your way – can you identify it? Self sabotage? Interruptions, or uncooperative family members or staff? Over committing? Take a few moments and try

How to Maximize 24 hours and Get More Done Effortlessly

to figure out what the block is and then address it. You may need some support to enhance your stick-to-it-ability.

Challenge #5: I don't know how. Help! There are professional organizers and productivity gurus out there who can help you, who are trained and experienced, including me. It takes an organization plan to get organized, and professionals can help you learn the system so you can organize the attic, your office and your life. While hosts on organization shows on TV can show you some tools you can use, remember that they have a crew doing the work for them. Your goal is to make it happen.

Our daily board
Try this quick daily organization tip for your office: Use a dry erase board (inexpensive and easy to get in an office supply retail shop). Every Monday, on one side of the board write what has to be done that week in a bulleted list. On the other side of the board, write Monday and from the larger list choose and copy three to four to-do's. Follow the same daily process for Tuesday and so on. Add to your weekly list ONLY if it absolutely can't wait. This approach helps you stay focused on what you want to accomplish by keeping it in plain sight all day.

Maybe, someday...
Lists are great tools when they are used to enhance productivity. But don't keep just one overall list of everything that you have to do as it can give you a false sense of urgency to get everything done NOW. Instead try separate lists for Personal, Errands, Home Projects, Business Projects and don't forget your "Maybe, Someday" list. It's where you maintain your ideas, dreams, things you might want to do someday and don't want to forget. You can draw from each list what needs to be done Today.

How to Maximize 24 hours and Get More Done Effortlessly

Office messes

Dear Paris: My office is a mess! I know that some people say that a messy desk is a sign of an organized mind, but I am telling you that's not me. My office mess is driving me crazy. Every time I try to start making some sense and order, the phone rings or there are more emails to answer or I get distracted by something I pick up to put away. Do I have an attention deficit problem or am I just doomed to live a messy work life? Help, from Office Disaster

Dear Office Disaster: Whoa! Time to take control of your work life, not just your office! You are letting people, machines and paper manage you instead of the other way around. It's time for an intervention, and I am the woman for the job. Call or e-mail me for a 7-point plan to get this turned around. Between now and then, ask yourself: Do I want to be a human doing or a human being? Looking forward to your call....

Who's the boss in your busy day? The clock, your clients, your e-mail account, your smart phone, your children, your partner, your in-laws? Take charge and get yourself back! It's time to organize your day your way and here are a few ideas for you:

List the top three things you plan to accomplish today. Stay focused on these three items, the most important first.

Instead of answering or reading texts and calls and emails as they come in, set aside an hour in the morning and an hour in the afternoon to do this work. This will help you avoid interruptions when you are trying to accomplish your tasks.

Don't let yourself make promises for doing things in a time frame that you already know will make you crazy stressed. Estimate when you can get something done and double it.

How to Maximize 24 hours and Get More Done Effortlessly

The important people in your life come first, but unless it is an emergency you are not a slave to them! Be cooperative and helpful, but draw the line and let others do what they are able.

How to Maximize 24 hours and Get More Done Effortlessly

Pros, cons and quick tips for your "Time Style"

Ever notice how some people seem to be doing many things at once, while others stick to just one thing at a time? Or how some people have a plan and others like to just let it happen?

Apparently, there's evidence that each of us has a time management personality and that no one time management tool works for everyone. From both my readings and my experience in helping people organize their time (note that we cannot manage time - we can only manage how we use it!) I've developed the styles below.

Here's a quick rundown on a few different time personalities - they are not mutually exclusive and you are most likely some combination of these five styles, although usually one is dominant.

The Planner
Plans ahead, uses to-do lists, everything on a set schedule, appointment book full, blank spaces on the schedule are meant to be filled in

If you want to share time with a planner, you better make an appointment

Pros: Things get done, usually on time to appointments/events, feels in control of time

Cons: Can be inflexible, obsessed with lists, change can cause anxiety

Tip: Plan for the unexpected

Last Seen: Adding an accomplished task to "to-do" list just to cross it off.

How to Maximize 24 hours and Get More Done Effortlessly

The Free Spirit
Tends to let the day flow as it comes into their lives, little planning, lives in the moment, likes the open spaces in the appointment book. If you want to share time with a free spirit, suggest a spur of the moment outing

Pros: Able to handle unexpected, great at putting out fires and handling problems

Cons: Often late to meetings, lacks sense of time limitations, can feel overwhelmed

Tip: Use a kitchen timer to help you become time aware

Last Seen: On the way to a new adventure

The NOW Spirit
Likes to get things done right now and quickly, little tolerance for small talk, task oriented and generally feels that any time not devoted to task at hand is wasted time.

If you want to share time with a now spirit, get to the point quickly and move on.

Pros: Can accomplish tasks in shorter amount of time than most, has sense of urgency

Cons: Can be perceived as abrupt, impatient, may miss important details in the rush

Tip: Use your waiting time to do something else productive to avoid impatience

Last Seen: Fuming in quick checkout line because customer had 7 items instead of 6

How to Maximize 24 hours and Get More Done Effortlessly

The Multitasker: Prefers to do more than one thing at a time, i.e.. talk on phone while answering emails or work on to-do list or project while in a meeting.

If you want to spend time with a multitasker, be sure to request their full attention

Pros: Gets a lot done, moves along various tasks incrementally.

Cons: Distraction means mistakes, quality of work can suffer due to lack of necessary attention.

Tip: Ask yourself- is it better to get one thing done well than three things done poorly?

Last seen: Seeking bionic extra arm attachments

The One Job Wonder
Focused on getting finished with one task before starting another. Does not allow distraction, usually produces quality work.

If you want to spend time with a one job wonder, be certain you are the task of the moment.

Pros: Pays attention to task at hand, completes projects.

Cons: Can be inflexible when unexpected arises, and may neglect other timely tasks.

Tip: Build time in your day for the unexpected.

Last seen: Working on project from last year, needs food and water

How to Maximize 24 hours and Get More Done Effortlessly

Keeping a Healthy You

Work Life Balance

You can use these five tips to plan a better split between professional and personal lives and ensure you give your best at home and on the job! Try planning a month at a time using these ideas to get started:

1. *Start with small steps*: Can you resist the temptation to check your business emails when you are away from the workplace? Try it for an hour to start and then increase by 15 minutes for several days.

This is a tough assignment for most - to make it easier, maintain separate home/work phone and email accounts. If you work from home, it helps to have a designated work place that you can walk away from at scheduled times.

2. *Tell it like it is*: Boundary setting is critical to your plan for a quality work and home life. Have a candid conversation with your manager and team about your boundaries. Negotiate what will work for you and your business or organization. Be open to team member's communication on the same topic. If a spouse and children are in the picture, be sure to communicate your boundaries there as well. Here's the hard part: hold those boundaries, but....

3. *...Be flexible*: Sometimes it pays to work longer or less - when there's a special project, a pending deadline, or when your child is playing in a soccer tournament. Use your judgment when you are making decisions to temporarily move those boundaries, but remember the move IS temporary.

How to Maximize 24 hours and Get More Done Effortlessly

4. *Ask yourself*: What is the worst that can happen if I don't finish this work now? (Hint...unless you are a real slacker, it's doubtful there is anything that can't wait a little while longer.) Who will be most adversely effected if I work late every night? (Hint... you, for one, but also partner or children at home). Why am I sacrificing a personal life for a work life? (Hint...maybe you are zoning out from real life issues through your work).

5. *Delegate it*: You can delegate to team members at the office, to your older children and your spouse, or to virtual assistants if you work at home. An "I have to do it all myself" mindset will ensure just that, with the added issue of self induced stress and no life outside of work.

Lastly, even if you love your work as many do, it's critical to unplug and make time for your personal growth and down time so that you can gain and give your business life the creativity and fresh energy needed to move forward.

What does Julie Morgenstern do when she has too much on her plate?

"When my workload swells to exceed the time I have available, I take a few minutes to step back, evaluate what's on my plate and strategize a way to streamline things to become more manageable, and ensure I am focusing on the highest and best use of my time. I use my 4Ds to lighten my load. The options are:

- **Delete** *tasks that are not worth the time invested.*

- **Delay** *tasks by rescheduling them for a more appropriate time.*

- **Diminish** *tasks by finding a more efficient way to get them done. (e.g a call vs a complicated email)*

How to Maximize 24 hours and Get More Done Effortlessly

- ***Delegate*** *tasks by giving them to someone who can do it better than me, faster than me, or good enough.*

The 4D's a part of my natural thought process—I apply them to all new requests, to daily planning, and to periodic Tune-ups to my schedule when things feel out of balance."
~ Julie Morgenstern, Organizing and Productivity expert and NY Times Bestselling author of 5 books, including ORGANIZING FROM THE INSIDE and TIME MANAGEMENT FROM THE INSIDE OUT www.juliemorgenstern.com

How to Maximize 24 hours and Get More Done Effortlessly

*W*ork hard, play hard, sleep fast

It's a phrase that has been a mantra for college students, an excuse for overwork in corporate culture, and even a song topic in country singer Gretchen Wilson's 2009 ditty *Work hard, play harder.*

During tough economic times everyone seems to be working harder to pick up the financial slack and the stress of financial challenges often results in playing harder, with little time left for rest.

Not such a good idea
Putting in long hours and working very hard as a way of life has its merits, of course, but there is a problem: it's also a certain road to burnout. Playing hard, in the form of burning the candle at both ends is also... a certain road to burnout. And the problem with sleeping fast...well, you get the picture.

Unless you want to come crashing to a halt in all areas of your life, work hard, play hard, sleep fast isn't the road to a productive and rewarding life. In fact, the science says your work deteriorates when you don't get perspective and rest. Evidence also indicates over work contributes to diabetes, cardiovascular problems, immune system weakening and obesity. And as for sleep, there is very strong support that sleep deprivation causes poor judgment, degraded memory, and on the job performance issues.

Work smarter, not harder

A better approach? Work smart. Believe it or not, you are not doing better work just because you work long hours.

Continue the year with a new philosophy that will make you more productive and healthier emotionally and physically.

How to Maximize 24 hours and Get More Done Effortlessly

"The first thing I have to do is push the pause button, stop and breathe. When that feeling of being overwhelmed starts to take hold, it's important to create space and clear the decks. At this point, I Can pick out the things that are more "busywork" that are distracting me and get them off my list by dropping them or outsourcing. I then prioritize the work that supports my focus goals, schedule them on my calendar and push play. It sounds counter-intuitive to stop when everything is pushing in, but it's the only way for me to get clarity and reconnect with my vision."
~~ Nicole Chamblin, *MA, CPO®*, of Visions Productivity Solutions

Here are some starter guidelines to help you begin your work smarter journey:

Streamline your work flow: Taking the time now to figure out where you are duplicating work, wasting time and just not efficient will pay off with higher productivity results. If you are running a business, you may need to get some professional help with this process, as an outsider can see things you can't.

Delegate: All those tasks that are non-income producing, boring, repetitive or you just aren't good at can be delegated to someone on your team or someone you contract with part time. For example, if you don't like to write, then contract with a copy writer to do it for you or have a staff or team member do the job, then you edit.

Plan ahead: Everything I've read about taking just a half hour a day to plan for the next day and week shows that this technique yields positive results. Your goal is to be the boss of your work, not your work be the boss of you.

Be proactive: Most work problems don't arrive unexpected. They start as a little thing, maybe an intuitive thought, or one disgruntled client, then grow. Don't wait until the problem is so large it becomes untenable. Catch it early or prevent it all together with a proactive rather than reactive stance.

How to Maximize 24 hours and Get More Done Effortlessly

Think before acting: Every action has a reaction, so think through your plans, programs and actions in business before you act. Assess risks and benefits quickly, and then make your decision.

How to Maximize 24 hours and Get More Done Effortlessly

Priorities

December is traditionally the month where you just want to clone yourself.

If only there were two of you – or even better, four of you – then you could take that work list, home list, and holiday happenings list then divide it up amongst yourself. Instead, you are trying to figure out what to do first and what to do next in order to act like a competent juggler and keep all those balls in the air.

"Like it or not, the world changes, priorities change and so do you." Merilu Henner Actress

Merilu Henner's quote, about how priorities change and so do you, might be a small tidbit but it looms large when taken with our ability to handle the world around us. Part of our problem with juggling the many things that need to be accomplished lies in the continued variables. Just about the time you figure out how you will do each thing, when you will do it and you start to feel better, someone throws one more ball into your mix. It might be a small ball but it throws you completely off balance. How will you possibly change everything you planned to fit in something new? It makes you crazy.

One of the best things you can do to stay calm and think logically. In a stressful, busy season like December recognize and accept that change is inevitable. The world changes. Circumstances change.

Priorities will need to change.

In other words, go with the flow.

How to Maximize 24 hours and Get More Done Effortlessly

Once, as a young mother, when I was to totally distraught over too much to do and too little time to do it in, I complained to my husband that I just wanted things to be normal again. He laughed and told me that "This is normal." It was not the answer that I wanted to hear but it was the truth.

Change is normal. Accept it.

So how do you manage priorities when so many variables that went into your decision making change? As you come upon January and a New Year, it is the perfect time to set priorities at work, at your home and for your personal life. You may have even set goals last year. It might be surprising to learn that some of those goals are the same and other goals you have are vastly different. That is pretty normal considering how much things change constantly.

Three Ways to Prioritize

Lists

"Oh bother," Winnie-the-Pooh might exclaim when confronted with a quote on organization. It might seem like you could just take off and do something – anything- instead of making lists. The problem with rushing about into this task or that task is you are likely to end up "all mixed up."

When confronted with too much to do, the best way to approach setting priorities is to create some lists. At any given time, you've a set of things to do for your job, another set to do for your home, a third set to do for your personal life and, most important, you've things you really need to do for yourself, from finding time to exercise to making time for important health checks.

Creating lists is a great way to prioritize. The act of listing each thing you need to do will bring about a sense of logic. There are certain things that must be done before other things can be accomplished. Want to sell your house? Fixing that leaky roof should come first. Want to get a promotion at work? Taking

How to Maximize 24 hours and Get More Done Effortlessly

responsibility for a new project will need to come first. Use your lists of things to do to help you prioritize.

Deadlines
The anxiety you feel by a looming deadline is actually a good thing. The adrenaline rush needed to push on and complete a goal comes along and slams into you. It propels you along.

Anytime you have an open-ended task, such as "One of these days I am finally going to paint the exterior of my house," it's just not going to happen. If you don't go to the paint store and get the paint, block out a weekend to actually do it and line up some help, you'll think about painting your house every time you pull in the driveway but it won't take place.

Sales goals at work exist for a reason. Semesters end with a report card for a reason. Diets start with and end with a goal weight for a reason. Deadlines work.

Take your to-do list and assign deadlines. Some items on your list come equipped with deadlines, such as paying taxes by April 15th or submitting your MBA application by closing date. Other items on your list require you to assign them a deadline. You need to establish a deadline for beginning the project as well as one to complete the project.

The assigned deadlines help you prioritize your to-do list.

Consider the YOU factor
When attacked by the too-much-to-do monster, you are likely to be spinning in a circle unsure of which way to go. It may remind you of the Wizard of Oz movie when the scarecrow gives directions by pointing to two directions at the same time and telling Dorothy to go that way.

How to Maximize 24 hours and Get More Done Effortlessly

Stephen Covey, best known for his hit book "The Seven Habits of Highly Effective People," is so right that you can't prioritize without saying "no." In essence, each time you say "yes," you are saying no to something. There isn't any way to be in two places at the same time or to do two things at the exact same moment.
So how do you decide which item gets the yes vote and which gets the no vote? That's where the YOU factor comes in. Remember those lists? Go back to your lists and note for each item if only YOU can do that item. I'm pretty sure that only YOU can go in and get blood work done to check your cholesterol! But I am also pretty sure that you can find someone to paint your house.

Getting things done doesn't always mean that YOU have to be the one doing them. If you mow your lawn or hire the neighborhood kid to mow your lawn, you can cross lawn off your to-do list. Either way it is done.

What items can you delegate at work? What items can you outsource? What items can only YOU do? Keep in mind that there are things you might really want to do, but this exercise is for you to identify the things that no one else can do for you. Highlighting these items is a great priority tool.

Organize. Deadlines. The YOU factor.

Just like the world changes, your day and week change, and so do your priorities, you'll have to change how you approach them. If you organize your to-do items into lists, study all deadlines and apply deadlines to those that don't have one and then use the YOU factor, you'll have a good grip on how to prioritize your time.

How to Maximize 24 hours and Get More Done Effortlessly

Delegation Might Save the Day – and You

It's great to have goals and set priorities. But, what happens when you simply can't get everything done despite priorities?

Realize that scenario will happen. At some point, push comes to shove and you are going to have to make some decisions.

Re-prioritize your list.

Ask yourself if there are any deadlines that can be moved. What would need to happen in order to make that work? Who would you need to involve in this decision? Move up to the top of your to-do list any action items involving changing deadlines – then return to focus on your priority.

Or, ask yourself if you can delegate? What can you move off of your plate? There is a right and wrong way to delegate at work. One tip is to focus your delegating on strengths and weaknesses of those you can delegate to. Instead of focusing on who isn't busy or who likes you and you can convince them to take the task, focus on who is really a good match for the task. If you do so, the task will get done. It is less likely it will bounce back on your desk or end up done incorrectly.

Need to Prioritize? Grab your Phone.

Seriously. You probably think that your phone actually detracts you from work. Between hanging out on social media, texts from friends and a constant stream of emails, you might feel your phone keeps you out-of-focus. That may be true but you can use your phone as an amazing tool to stay organized and prioritized.

How to Maximize 24 hours and Get More Done Effortlessly

There are over 100 apps devoted to prioritizing. There is a terrific tool for figuring out the right one for you at AppCrawlr, the app discover engine.

The search engine at AppCrawlr allows you to decide if you want to search only free apps or paid apps. Beyond price, the search engine allows you to narrow down your focus by choosing categories, topics, how you want it to help you, what audience fits you best and what features you want. For example, you could choose that you want to manage to-do lists and tasks, you want help staying organized, you are a small business person and also a busy mom and you'd like one that features a sync to your calendar.

Ta da! The AppCrawlr led our search to Weave, a free app that helps you "stay in control" of your life and business. Use AppCrawlr to find an app to help you prioritize.

Align Your Priorities with Your Goals
While on the surface, it seems like matching your priorities with your goals would be a given. But, on closer inspection, is that really true for you?

An easy check to see if you are in alignment is to grab a pen and paper for a quick exercise. On the front of your paper, make a list of the five things that you spend the most time doing. What really eats up your time? Is it emails? Phone calls? Research? Filing? Playing janitor and trying to keep things in order?

Next, flip your paper over and make a totally new list. Erase that first list from your mind. Now make a list of the five things you LOVE about your job or career. What things make you excited about the day? What do you wish you could do more of? What are you really, really good at?

How to Maximize 24 hours and Get More Done Effortlessly

Now compare the two lists. Is there anything on the two lists that are the same? While we all have to do a few things we are not fond of, ideally your lists should have quite a few matches.

Is the time you are spending leading you to the job or life you really want? Taking an honest look at how you spend your time verses how you want to spend your time is a great way to set new priorities.

ACKNOWLEDGEMENTS

A SPECIAL THANKS TO MY WONDERFUL PRODUCTIVITY COLLEAGUES

~~ Cena Block, founder of SaneSpaces.com and the creator of the Time & Space Style Inventory™ (TSSI™) Author of TIME TO TOSS IT: GET UNCLUTTERED AND ORGANIZED! AND GETTING IT ALL DONE IN THE UNSTOPPABLE WOMAN'S GUIDE TO EMOTIONAL WELL BEING

~~ Nicole Chamblin, *MA, CPO®*, of Visions Productivity Solutions, is a productivity speaker and consultant *who loves helping clients connect with their vision, communicate their goals and collaborate with others more productively.* www.visionsps.com

~~ Barbara Hemphill, Founder, Productive Environment Institute Author of LESS CLUTTER MORE LIFE www.ProductiveEnvironment.com

~~Julie Morgenstern, Organizing and Productivity expert and NY Times Bestselling author of 5 books, including ORGANIZING FROM THE INSIDE and TIME MANAGEMENT FROM THE INSIDE OUT www.juliemorgenstern.com

~~ Lisa Montanaro is a Productivity Consultant, Success Coach, Business Strategist, Speaker, Author. She helps clients and audiences Create Your Purpose & Live Your Passion. www.LisaMontanaro.com

How to Maximize 24 hours and Get More Done Effortlessly

Thank you for purchasing this book! I hope it inspires and motivates you to increase your efficiency. It is my desire that you enhance your productivity and efficiency in life and in business.

For additional resources and assistance visit www.ParisLoveProductivityInstitute.com

To Your Productivity

Paris

How to Maximize 24 hours and Get More Done Effortlessly